TEN OF THE BEST MYTHS

GIANT
S T O R I E S

W

FRANKLIN WATTS
LONDON • SYDNEY

First published in the UK in 2014 by Franklin Watts

Franklin Watts
338 Euston Road
London NW1 3BH

Franklin Watts Australia
Level 17/207 Kent Street
Sydney, NSW 2000

Dewey classification: 398.2'1

A CIP catalogue record for this book is available from the British Library.

ISBN: 978 1 4451 3211 2

Franklin Watts is a division of Hachette Children's Books, an Hachette UK company.
www.hachette.co.uk

TEN OF THE BEST MYTHS GIANT STORIES
was produced for Franklin Watts by
David West Children's Books, 6 Princeton Court, 55 Felsham Road, London SW15 1AZ

Designed and illustrated by David West
Contributing editor: Steve Parker

Printed in China

THE STORIES

Cabracan

Cabracan was a Mayan giant who destroyed mountains. He was the son of Vucub-Caquix, an evil giant bird-god. This is the story of how the hero twins, Hunahpu and Xbalanque, defeated Cabracan.

Cabracan the giant was going about his business as usual – shaking the land and destroying mountains. Quaking the Earth made him feel good and he boasted about his greatness. This annoyed the gods and so they asked the twins, Hunahpu and Xbalanque, to put an end to the giant's boastfulness.

The two brothers set off in the direction of the trembling and quaking. They soon found Cabracan.

"Where are you going, great shaker?" they asked him.

Blowguns are long tubes which shoot poisonous darts by blowing them through the tube. Mayans used them to hunt animals.

"Nowhere," he answered. "I am staying to shake these mountains to the ground. Why are you here?"

"We are hunters," they replied. "We are on our way to a huge mountain where the Sun rises. Many birds are there to shoot with our blowguns."

"A huge mountain, you say?" asked Cabracan, interested. "Take me there and I will shake it to the ground!"

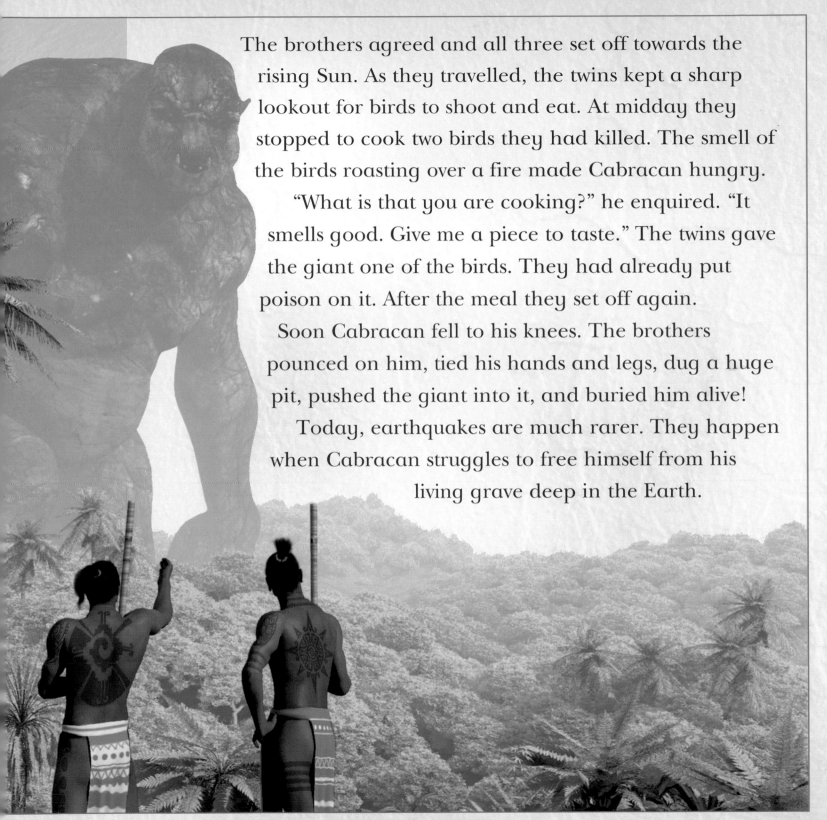

The brothers agreed and all three set off towards the rising Sun. As they travelled, the twins kept a sharp lookout for birds to shoot and eat. At midday they stopped to cook two birds they had killed. The smell of the birds roasting over a fire made Cabracan hungry.

"What is that you are cooking?" he enquired. "It smells good. Give me a piece to taste." The twins gave the giant one of the birds. They had already put poison on it. After the meal they set off again.

Soon Cabracan fell to his knees. The brothers pounced on him, tied his hands and legs, dug a huge pit, pushed the giant into it, and buried him alive!

Today, earthquakes are much rarer. They happen when Cabracan struggles to free himself from his living grave deep in the Earth.

Ferragut

Ferragut was a Saracen warrior of enormous size. This descendent of Goliath had such thick skin that no blade could penetrate it.

The giant Ferragut had been sent to Nájera in Spain by the **Emir** of Babylon, to fight the Christian army of Charlemagne. Ferragut feared neither dagger, sword nor lance, and he had the strength of forty men.

Charlemagne, the king of the **Franks**, sent several of his champions to fight the giant. But he defeated all of them easily. Eventually the hero, Roland, met with Ferragut to do battle.

*"Saracens" was the name for Muslims used in Europe during the **medieval** era. Many battles were fought between Christian armies and Muslim armies during this time.*

For two days the hero and the giant fought each other. But Roland could not find a way of wounding his foe. At night the two stopped fighting to rest. But Ferragut had difficulty sleeping since he had no pillow upon which to rest his head. So, on the second night, Roland found a smooth, flat rock and kindly placed it under the sleeping giant's head.

The next morning, Ferragut was very taken with Roland's courteous behaviour. He engaged him in conversation as they ate their breakfast. It was during this talk that the giant, by accident, mentioned his weak spot. "I am invulnerable to sword and arrow – except in my navel," he revealed.

It was Ferragut's undoing. As they resumed combat, Roland dealt a death blow to the giant's navel and he fell to the ground, dead.

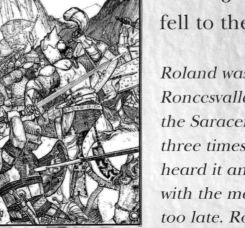

Roland was killed at the battle of Roncesvalles, fighting against the Saracens. He blew his horn three times before Charlemagne heard it and rushed to his rescue with the main army. But it was too late. Roland had died.

Finn McCool

Finn McCool was a giant warrior of Irish mythology. He also appeared in the mythologies of Scotland and the Isle of Man. He is sometimes described as a giant with white hair. "Finn" is actually a nickname, meaning fair or light-haired.

One day, as Finn was going about his regular business, a Scottish giant named Fingal began to shout insults at him across the Irish Sea. In anger, Finn lifted a lump of land and threw it at Fingal. It landed in the sea with a massive splash, creating the Isle of Man.

Fingal just laughed and hurled a few more insults at Finn. This made the Irish giant even more angry. In his rage he started throwing rocks into the sea to build a road, called a causeway, all the way to Scotland. It took him a week to finish. But in the meantime Fingal had grown bored. He wandered off to find someone else to insult.

Northern Ireland

Scotland

Ireland

Isle of Man

Wales England

The Isle of Man is in the Irish Sea, at the geographical centre of the British Isles.

After finishing the causeway, Finn was very tired. Since there was no sign of Fingal, he returned home for a well-earned rest. He was just about to put his head on the pillow when the ground began to tremble. It was Fingal crossing the causeway that Finn had just built!

"I am too tired to fight," said Finn to his wife. She replied, "Don't worry dear, I have an idea."

So she dressed him in baby clothes and put him in a large crib.

When Fingal arrived at Finn's house, Finn's wife welcomed him. "My husband will be back soon. Will you not come in and wait?" she asked politely.

On entering the house, Fingal saw the massive crib with Finn lying in it. "What's in there?" he enquired.

"Oh, that's our baby, little Finn," replied the wife.

"My goodness!" thought Fingal, worried. "If that's his baby, how huge is Finn himself?"

Fingal quickly devised a new plan. "I must be away the noo," he cried. "I have just remembered, I left the stove burning unattended!"

With that, Fingal ran back to his home in Scotland. On the way he tore up the causeway behind him, so that Finn could never follow.

The Giant's Causeway, made of 40,000 six-sided columns of rock, is a real place on the north-east coast of Northern Ireland.

9

Geryon

Geryon was a monstrous giant of ancient Greek mythology who owned a herd of magnificent red cattle. He had one body, three heads, six arms and six legs.

Before the famous Greek hero Heracles could live forever, he had to complete twelve tasks, or labours, for King Eurystheus. His tenth labour was to steal the cattle of the giant Geryon. This huge, fearsome warrior lived on the isle of Eurytheia, far from King Eurystheus' court.

After travelling through a desert for many days, Heracles became angry at the heat and his lack of progress. In frustration, he fired an arrow at Helios, the sun god. Helios was impressed with Heracles' courage and allowed him to board his Golden Cup, in which he crossed the sky daily from east to west. Thus, Heracles quickly arrived on the Eurytheia shore.

Cerberus, the three-headed hell-hound guarded the gates of the Underworld, to prevent prisoners escaping. The watchdog, Orthrus, was his brother.

Immediately, Heracles was attacked by the guardians of the cattle: the two-headed hound Orthrus and the herder Eurytion. With one huge blow from his olive-wood club, Heracles killed both the watchdog and the herder. But as he gathered the cattle, the ground shook. In the distance appeared the towering shape of Geryon, moving towards him with enormous strides.

Heracles strung his bow and fired an arrow dipped in the poisonous blood of the **Hydra**. The arrow struck Geryon in the forehead. No man, nor god, nor giant, could survive that terrible venom. Geryon crashed to the ground, stone dead. Heracles captured the cattle and so completed his tenth labour.

On Heracles' return, some of the cattle were stolen by the fire-breathing giant Cacus. Heracles found him hiding in a cave with the animals, and clubbed him to death.

Goliath

*Goliath was a giant **Philistine** warrior whose story appears in the Bible.*

King Saul of Israel and his army faced the Philistine army near the Valley of Elah. The champion of the Philistines was the giant Goliath. For forty days, twice each day, he strode forwards from his army lines to challenge the Israelites.

"Who will fight me to decide which side is the victor?" he called out.

Goliath was a mountain of a man, standing 3 metres (9.8 feet) tall. So King Saul and all the Israelite army were afraid.

A sling is an ancient weapon that effectively makes the arm longer. It fires a stone like a bullet, at speeds of 30 metres (100 ft) per second, over distances of 400 metres (1300 ft).

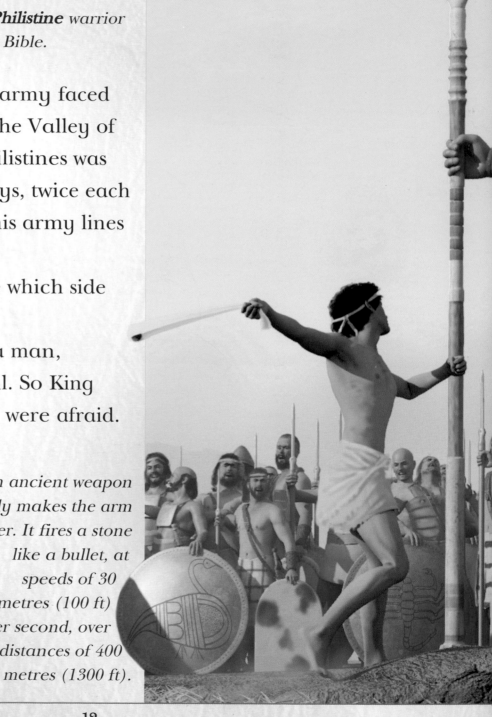

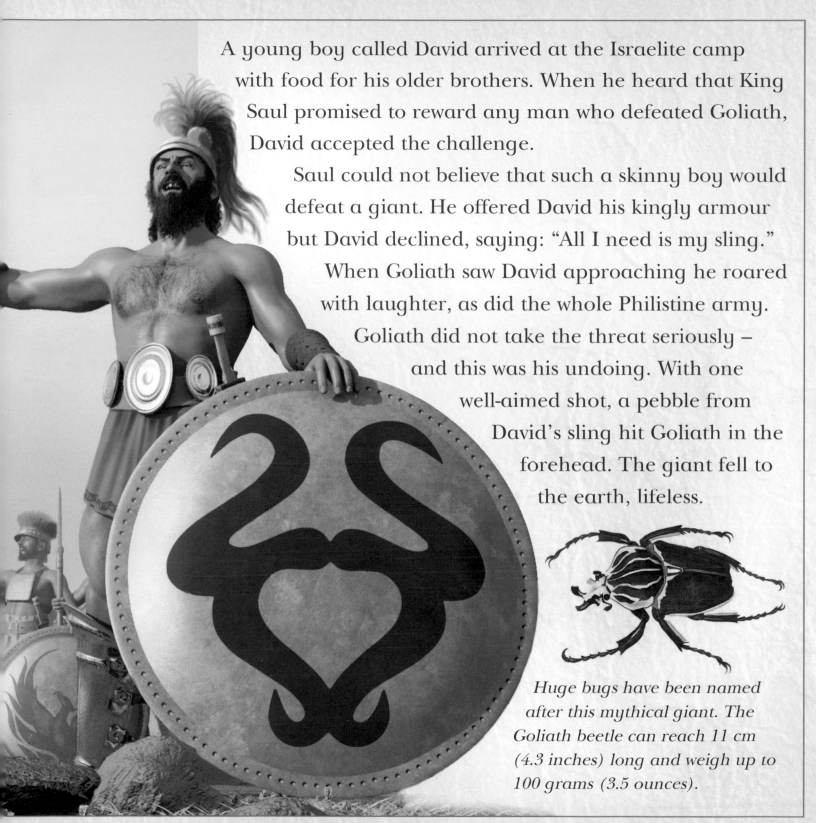

A young boy called David arrived at the Israelite camp with food for his older brothers. When he heard that King Saul promised to reward any man who defeated Goliath, David accepted the challenge.

Saul could not believe that such a skinny boy would defeat a giant. He offered David his kingly armour but David declined, saying: "All I need is my sling." When Goliath saw David approaching he roared with laughter, as did the whole Philistine army. Goliath did not take the threat seriously – and this was his undoing. With one well-aimed shot, a pebble from David's sling hit Goliath in the forehead. The giant fell to the earth, lifeless.

Huge bugs have been named after this mythical giant. The Goliath beetle can reach 11 cm (4.3 inches) long and weigh up to 100 grams (3.5 ounces).

Kumbhakarna

In the Indian Ramayana epic, Kumbhakarna – younger brother of Ravana – was a giant with a huge appetite.

The ground shook like an earthquake. Workers toiling in the fields looked round to see a monstrous giant rising from the Earth. Dust and stones poured off him. It was Kumbhakarna, rising wearily from his six-month slumber.

The giant was hungry, and the people knew. They ran in terror. Kumbhakarna snatched up and devoured the slowest. He would eat many of them before the day ended and he returned to his half-year sleep.

Saraswati is the Hindu goddess of knowledge, music, arts and science. She possesses four arms, and is usually shown wearing a spotless white sari.

"How did Kumbhakarna get to this state?" you ask.

It was said that Kumbhakarna was so pious, intelligent and brave that Indra, leader of the gods, was jealous of him. When Kumbhakarna asked for a boon (blessing) from Brahma, god of creation, his tongue was cursed by the goddess Saraswati – acting on Indra's request.

So Kumbhakarna, instead of asking for what he wanted, requested to go to sleep. His wish was granted. Then his brother Ravana asked Brahma to undo this boon, since it was really an evil spell. As a compromise, Brahma allowed Kumbhakarna to wake for one day every six months.

Kumbhakarna's brother Ravana wanted to help in the war against Rama. He drove 1,000 elephants over the slumbering giant before he awoke. But Rama eventually won the battle.

Polyphemus the Cyclops

In Greek mythology Polyphemus, the gigantic one-eyed son of Poseidon, was a member of the Cyclops clan.

On his journey home from Troy, Greek hero Odysseus landed on the island of the Cyclops to look for food and water. He and his men entered a cave where they discovered massive bowls and plates. Suddenly huge sheep were herded into the cave – followed by a giant with one eye. It was a Cyclops. As the last sheep entered, the giant pushed a large boulder across to seal the entrance.

Odysseus emerged with his men from their hiding place.

"What is this? Strangers in my home!" shouted the Cyclops, tending his fire.

Odysseus bowed and, relying on the custom of hospitality, announced: "Our humblest apologies. We are travellers in search of provisions. I am Odysseus and these are my men."

The Cyclops replied, "Pah! My name is Polyphemus and I am hungry." Without warning he grabbed two of the men and began to eat them!

Of the many one-eyed creatures in legend, the child from Japan called a Hitotsume-kozo is perhaps the strangest. It appears suddenly and surprises people – yet is harmless.

In the morning, the Cyclops ate another two humans and left the cave with his sheep, pushing the boulder back over the entrance. That day, Odysseus made a plan and organised his men. The next night, as the Cyclops lay sleeping, Odysseus and the other survivors drove a large wooden spike into Polyphemus' eye, blinding him. The Cyclops screamed in pain but could not see to retaliate. The next morning as Polyphemus let out the sheep, he felt with his hands for anyone riding on them. Cunningly, Odysseus and his men escaped – by tying themselves to the sheep's undersides.

As Odysseus sailed off with his men, he boastfully called out his name. Unseeing Polyphemus threw huge rocks towards the sound, but he narrowly missed the escaping ship.

Sedna

In Inuit mythology, Sedna is the goddess of the sea and marine animals.

At the beginning of the world, there were giants. They lived on the land and ate the plants growing there. One day a baby girl was born and her giant parents named her Sedna.

Each day Sedna grew bigger. The larger she became, the more she ate. Eventually she was greater in size than her parents. Soon there was not enough food – Sedna had eaten all the plants. The giants were becoming hungry.

The Inuit hunt seals in kayaks, small canoes made from animal skins wrapped around a wooden frame.

One night Sedna's parents woke up screaming. She was trying to eat their legs! It was the last straw. They carried Sedna out to sea in their kayak and dropped her in the icy ocean. But when they tried to paddle back to land, the kayak would not move. Sedna was hanging on and the kayak was in danger of tipping over.

"We will both drown if we do not do something!" wailed Sedna's mother. The father took out his knife and started to cut off his daughter's fingers. As these fell into the sea, they turned into swimming creatures. One was a whale, another a seal. The fingers became all the animals of the sea.

With her fingers gone, Sedna sank to the bottom of the ocean. Here the animals built her a home. She now lives in a deep, wintery, watery world, where ice forms a crust far above.

Whenever the Inuit are short of food, they call on Sedna – and she provides it.

In 2003, a new space object was discovered beyond the farthest planet, Neptune. It was a dwarf planet and this red, icy world was named Sedna after the Inuit goddess.

Skrymir

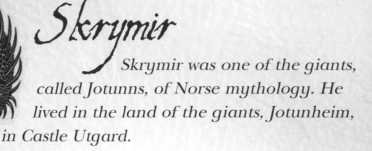

Skrymir was one of the giants, called Jotunns, of Norse mythology. He lived in the land of the giants, Jotunheim, in Castle Utgard.

One day the giant-bashing god Thor, and the trickster god Loki, found themselves in the home of Skrymir. The giant had lured them to Castle Utgard by trickery.

"Now that you two gods are here," said Skrymir, in his great hall full of giants, "you must entertain us with feats of strength."

Loki went first, but he lost an eating contest with the giant Logi. Next Skrymir turned to Thor, asking, "Perhaps a drinking contest?" A drinking horn was brought forward. "A good drinker could down this in one go!" claimed Skrymir.

Thor gulped and gulped but the amount of drink hardly changed.

Skrymir smiled. "Pah! Not such a big drinker after all. Why not try to lift this large cat off the ground?"

Thor had a magic hammer and belt that doubled his strength.

Thor could barely lift one paw of the cat from the ground. He gave up exhausted, but by now he was in a rage. "I can defeat any of you in a fight!" he shouted.

Skrymir laughed and suggested he fought an old woman, who had taken up a wrestling stance. Thor grabbed her and tried to throw her, but again he had no effect. Skrymir brought the contest to an end and allowed the two gods to sleep. Next morning Skrymir took Thor and Loki to the edge of Jotunheim. Thor was miserable. How could he hold up his head in front of the other gods? Skrymir let them into his secret. "We giants had heard of your strength, so we were unwilling to pit ourselves against you. The drinking horn was attached to the ocean and you actually lowered it. The cat was really the Midgard serpent, which is so big it circles the Earth. Finally, the woman was old age. And no one can defeat old age."

In Norse mythology there will be a great battle, called Ragnarok, between the gods and the giants. It will signal the end of the world. Then a new Earth will be created.

Talos

Talos was a bronze giant forged by Hephaestus, the Greek god of blacksmiths, for chief god Zeus. Talos was sent by Zeus to guard Europa, a Phoenician princess, who lived on the island of Crete.

Jason and his Argonauts were on their way back to Iolcus, after a successful quest to capture the Golden Fleece for King Pelias. With them was the sorceress Medea, who had used magic to help Jason with his quest. It had been a long and dangerous journey. Jason decided to stop at the island of Crete to take food and water on board their ship, *Argo*.

As they approached the island they heard a screeching, as if metal was rubbing against metal. It quickly became louder. Then, from behind a hill, appeared a towering figure of rusting bronze.

The myth of the Golden Fleece may have come from a type of early gold panning. Sheep fleeces, stretched over a wood frame, were submerged in a stream. Gold flecks floating past would collect in the wool. The fleeces were then hung in trees to dry, before the gold was shaken or combed out.

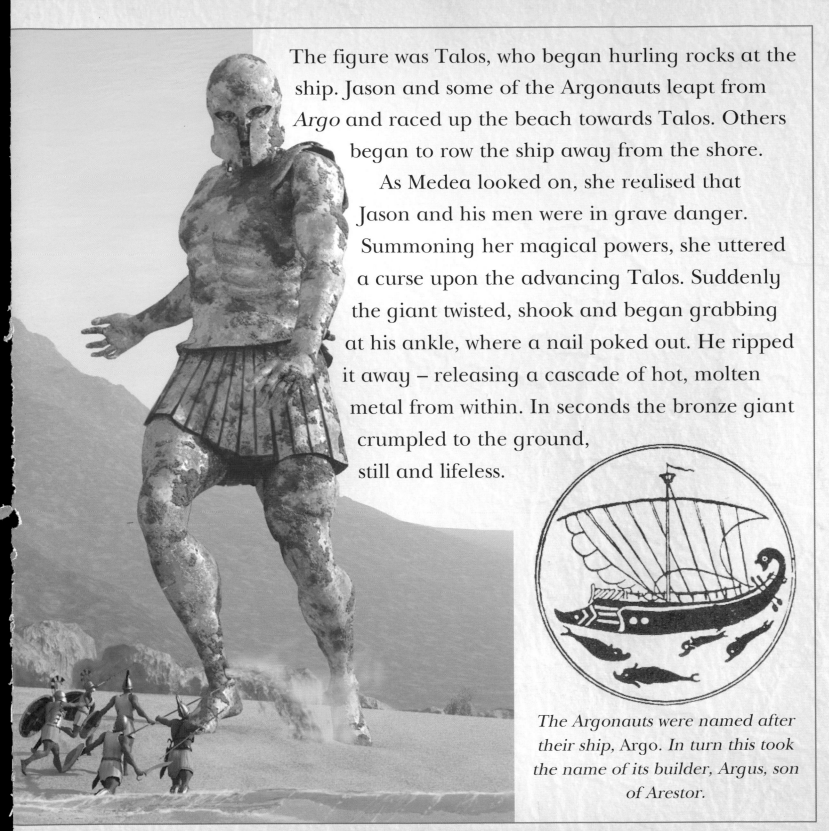

The figure was Talos, who began hurling rocks at the ship. Jason and some of the Argonauts leapt from *Argo* and raced up the beach towards Talos. Others began to row the ship away from the shore.

As Medea looked on, she realised that Jason and his men were in grave danger. Summoning her magical powers, she uttered a curse upon the advancing Talos. Suddenly the giant twisted, shook and began grabbing at his ankle, where a nail poked out. He ripped it away – releasing a cascade of hot, molten metal from within. In seconds the bronze giant crumpled to the ground, still and lifeless.

The Argonauts were named after their ship, Argo. *In turn this took the name of its builder, Argus, son of Arestor.*

GLOSSARY

Emir A title for governors or rulers used in the Muslim world.

Franks Originally members of a Germanic people. In the Middle Ages, Franks ruled most of western Europe.

Hydra A mythical Greek many-headed serpent whose heads grew again after they were cut off.

medieval The period of European history from the 5th to 15th centuries.

Philistines In ancient times, people of what became southern Palestine. They fought with the Israelites during the 11th and 12th centuries BCE.

INDEX